CITY OF WOODEN HOUSES GEORGETOWN, GUYANA

Compton Davis

CITY OF WOODEN HOUSES GEORGETOWN, GUYANA

MERRELL
LONDON · NEW YORK

CONTENTS

FOREWORD
DAVID A. GRANGER PRESIDENT OF THE COOPERATIVE REPUBLIC OF GUYANA

The City of Georgetown, the capital of the Cooperative Republic of Guyana, was founded 235 years ago. French republican revolutionary forces, under the command of Admiral the Comte de Kersaint, captured the former Dutch colony of Demerara from the English on 3 February 1782. The French established a centre called La Nouvelle Ville, or Long Champs. They soon handed Demerara back to the Dutch, who, on 14 September 1784, renamed the centre Stabroek.

The English took possession of the colony again on 22 April 1796 and later renamed Stabroek Georgetown. The English continued to hold the colonies of Demerara-Essequibo and Berbice (except for a brief interruption in 1802–3), up to 26 May 1966, when Guyana gained its Independence.

A distinctive indigenous architectural form evolved in Georgetown over the years, enhancing the skyline with numerous elegant buildings. These, typically, were two-storeyed wooden structures with louvred windows, jalousies, verandas and porticoes with high roofs and decorative fretwork designs. According to one writer:

> A traveller today can still enjoy streetscapes of great grace – broad avenues lined with samaan trees, which stand tall against white-painted wooden houses built in the colonial subtropical style. There is a profusion of architectural styles in the city, ranging from Gothic to semi-Tudor, Romanesque to Italian Renaissance, and the remarkable feature of the buildings is that they are virtually all made of wood.
>
> The wood used by the British was a mixture of hardy local greenheart and pine imported from North America … And the colony's prosperity attracted a number of enterprising architects …

Georgetown is still noted for its wooden churches, cinemas, cottages, municipal markets, offices, police stations, schools and other public buildings. This book is a valuable testament to Guyana's unique architectural heritage.

FOREWORD

DR JAMES ROSE DIRECTOR, DEPARTMENT OF CULTURE, GUYANA

The foundation of the future stands firmly on the achievements of the past. This historical adage holds seminal truth for building construction and house structures that have evolved and are evolving within our society. This book presents a photographic display of houses, the history of houses, historical houses and the history of development trends in the construction of homes, and showcases, as well, the skills and techniques employed by builders since the beginning of settlement times.

In today's world we are blessed with an amazing array of developments in science, technology and innovation, as well as high-grade building machinery, equipment and materials. It is therefore exceptionally easy to underestimate the early creations of those imaginative humans who, with but scant access to sciences and the arts, grappled with the vagaries of nature and provided us with the various forms of social habitation that we, the people of Guyana, have inherited.

Whether we are sensitive enough to recognize these efforts or not, the historical fact is that the seeds of our current lifestyles were sown by previous generations of social creators, and it is exceedingly beneficial and productive to revisit and help to keep alive the history of such creations and to draw new inspiration from these abodes of earlier ingenuity. This book both explicitly and implicitly recognizes and celebrates the notion that our ancestors, in spite of their manifold handicaps and various constraints, were ingenious enough to devise their own techniques to harness the bounty of Nature and produce magnificent edifices for which this country is famous and of which we as a people are very proud.

I feel privileged to have been asked by Mr Compton Davis to contribute to his book, which is not only a very exciting read but also a most valuable contribution to the social historiography of Guyana. It is an important reminder that, long before the Dutch constructed the first unembellished and undecorated cottage in the interior lands of Guyana, our Amerindian brothers and sisters had planted their benabs: simple, sparingly adorned, environmentally friendly, providing basic shelter from the elements and a central meeting place for the family. The cottages would expand with the decision to settle, and with the accumulation of wealth the great houses looked down on the long rages or logies that both accommodated and physically differentiated the social groupings in plantation society.

When towns and cities emerged and evolved on the low coastal strip, which was frequently inundated, these houses were raised above the ground on stilts. This afforded protection from flood waters, snakes and other creepy-crawlies, while also providing visual prominence to the building on its approach. Because it was available and, for the most part, affordable, wood was used to construct the houses. Just as the terrain influenced the model, so too did the building material: wood could easily be set afire, so sad experience dictated that the kitchen be set apart, initially detached, then separated by a pantry.

Guyana is fortunate in being less vulnerable to the natural disasters – hurricanes, destructive earthquakes and floods – that have ravaged so much of the human habitation of the neighbouring Caribbean and Latin America. But other, man-made, forces have had an effect: personal wealth; the pressure of urban and commercial development; vandalism; and fire. Reflecting much of this social genesis and more, Compton Davis has produced, in his book, a first and excellent photographic summary of the style and history of houses in Guyana. He showcases the various pressures that have influenced the country's construction patterns, especially as reflected in house-building. This book presents a fascinating photographic journey, exploring the valiant and creative efforts of past builders and engineers to develop innovative safe and sound habitation, and is a most welcome addition to the literature, whether as a collector's item or as a reference piece.

INTRODUCTION
GEORGETOWN AND ITS BUILDING TRADITION

The old wooden buildings of Georgetown, the capital of Guyana (formerly British Guiana), are characteristic of what has come to be known as Guyanese architecture. Classic examples of these buildings include the spectacular St George's Cathedral – famously one of the tallest wooden buildings in the world – Government House and the High Court with its mock-Tudor external wooden frame. However, the core of Guyanese architecture comprises numerous smaller, more prosaic buildings. It is these unassuming buildings that are the focus of this book.

At its most basic, Guyanese architecture can be described as colonial in style. The French, Dutch, Spanish and British all brought with them their respective local vernacular and the classic language and formal style of contemporary eighteenth- and nineteenth-century European architecture, with its emphasis on proportion, rhythm and decoration. These elements were reinterpreted by local craftsmen and constructed in wood. It was the British – the most influential and the final colonists – who, while developing the cities and plantations, brought the distinctive style that they were able to impose in the absence of a local vernacular. Instead of using stone and brick, they constructed churches, cathedrals, markets, railway stations and dwelling houses from the bountiful local supply of wood. The overall appearance is extraordinary and original, and echoes this complex lineage.

The photographs in this book are a visual reminder of the elegant colonial city that Georgetown once was, and also a tribute to the Guyanese builders and craftsmen who helped to shape it. Georgetown's old architecture reveals influences from Europe, Asia and Africa, adapted to create unique buildings suited to the landscape and climate of Guyana. The wide tree-lined avenues and boulevards flanked by elegant whitewashed colonial houses were the hallmark of the city, and, although somewhat less grand nowadays, still are: tourists and visitors are always enthused and inspired by these gems, and spurred to enquire about and explore the rich cultural heritage of Guyana epitomized by the colonial architecture of Georgetown.

Most of the foundations of the urban layout and architectural legacy of modern Georgetown were planned and built in the nineteenth and early twentieth centuries. However, the elegant white wooden buildings, along with the boulevards and open spaces that earned Georgetown the unofficial title 'garden city of the Caribbean', are rapidly disappearing. Since the mid-1980s, when the earliest of the photographs in this book were taken, a profound change has occurred. Many colonial houses have been destroyed by fire, decay and, more recently, demolition, and the slow creep of modernism is reflected in the glass-and-concrete buildings – apartment blocks, shopping malls, offices – that are rapidly replacing them. These photographs are therefore a visual historical document, depicting a building culture that is vanishing from the city of Georgetown.

Pages 14–15
Part of the 450-kilometre-long sea wall that protects Georgetown from the Atlantic Ocean. The wall owes its origins to the Dutch settlers, who in the seventeenth century began building the canals and reclaiming land for farming. Constructed piecemeal over many centuries, it was finally completed to form a comprehensive sea defence by the British government in the 1950s.

Below
The wide vista of Camp Street on a sunny day after a heavy downpour.

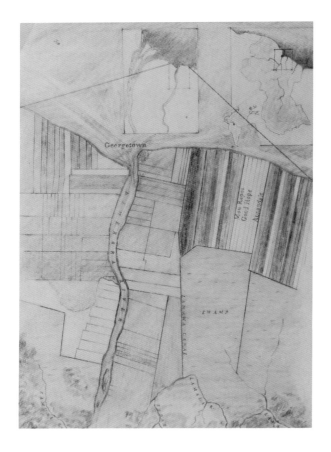

Georgetown is on the northeastern coast of Guyana, with Venezuela to the north, Brazil to the south and west, and Suriname to the southeast. The city is at the mouth of the Demerara River, facing the Atlantic Ocean. It is part of the river's flood plain, and this position and topography have dominated the development of its culture and architecture.

THE ORIGINS OF GEORGETOWN

In 1891 the English botanist and historian James Rodway (in *History of British Guiana, from the Year 1668 to the Present Time*) described Georgetown as a 'narrow strip' of land that

> *lies within a coastal plain that covers an area of approximately 1750 square miles out of a total landmass of over 3000 square miles. The coastal plain is about 40 miles deep and extends from the Courantyne River, to the east, and to the west the Demerara River where Georgetown is located. Around 80 per cent of Guyana's population live on the coastal belt where 80 per cent of its wealth and agriculture is produced. Much of the land lies at sea level, while some areas are four feet below high tide.*

Georgetown is on the delta of the Demerara River, one of the largest rivers in South America. It is backed by the tropical rainforest of the continent, and faces the Atlantic Ocean; the next land mass is Africa. The delta is by its nature flat and muddy and the climate hot, humid and rainy. Plantations, first of cotton and later of sugar, were built on reclaimed land in the seventeenth century with the arrival of the Spanish, and that continued for more than 100 years, during which time the Dutch, the French and the British settled.

In the first half of the eighteenth century the original settlers, the Dutch, established a base on Borsselen Island, 17 miles up the Demerara River, from which to administer the new colony. Elevating buildings had been an early solution to the development of swampy areas – indeed, there is evidence that the original Amerindian inhabitants did just that, sometimes raising entire villages on tree stumps – but if land near the coast was to be cultivated, it first had to be reclaimed from the mangrove swamps and the sea. With their experience of their own low-lying country, the Dutch set about tackling the problem. To keep out the sea they

KINGSTON

CUMMINGSBURG

ROBBSTOWN

WERK-EN-RUST

CHARLESTOWN

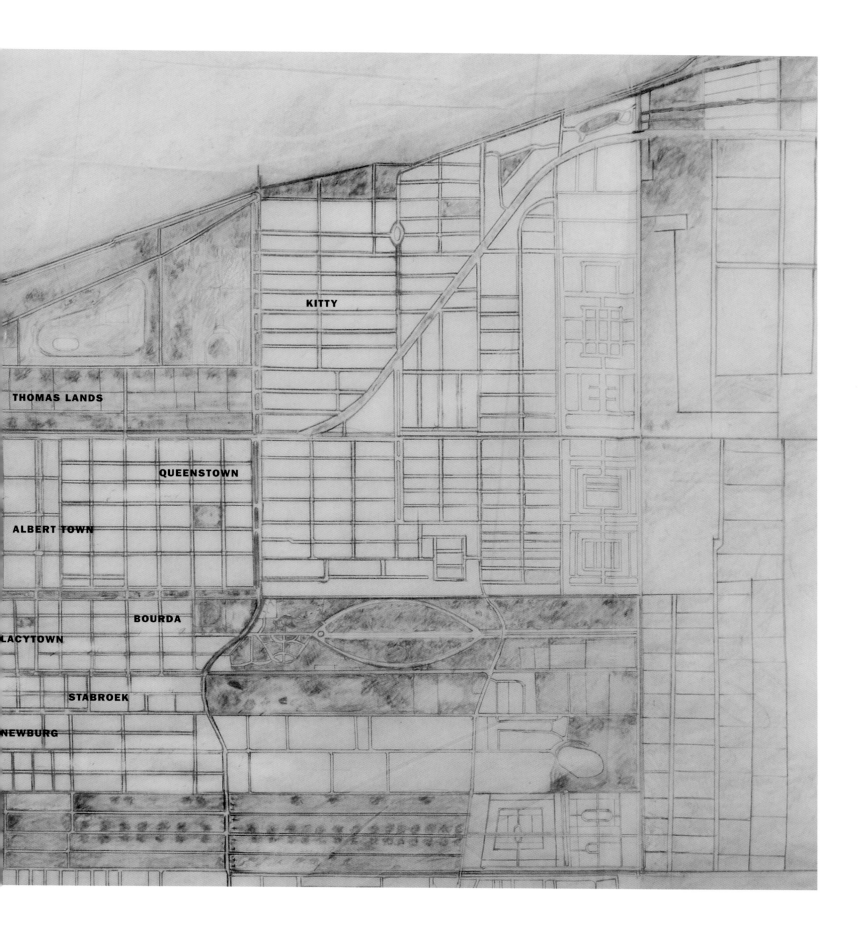

KITTY

THOMAS LANDS

QUEENSTOWN

ALBERT TOWN

BOURDA

LACYTOWN

STABROEK

NEWBURG

constructed a series of trenches, ditches and kokers, as well as several dams to control the small creeks that flowed into the rivers. Areas of plain were encircled with a profusion of walls. Once it was drained, the Dutch named the area Stabroek, with the intention of making it an administrative centre.

By 1759 it had become obvious that the settlement at Borsselen was not ideal for managing a growing colony, since many of the commercial activities and expanding plantations were located on reclaimed land closer to the mouth of the river. In spite of many attempts to hold back the water, flooding was a constant threat nearer the coast. Water was as likely to come pouring through breaches in the sea wall as to overflow from the rivers behind the dams. Sections of poorly maintained sea defence would break down, with inevitable loss of life and land. Indeed, a study of old maps of the Demerara region indicates several changes in plantation boundaries as the waters of the Atlantic flooded in.

A frenzied power struggle for control of the territory settled along the Atlantic coast and river inlets culminated in its ultimate cession to the British, and in 1814, under the Treaty of Utrecht (after the defeat of Napoleon in Europe), Britain was given sovereignty of the territory, which was then known as British Guiana. Stabroek was renamed Georgetown in homage to the incumbent monarch at the time. The colony remained a British overseas possession until it gained independence in 1966, when it changed its name to Guyana. On 23 February 1970 it officially became a republic.

Throughout the years of colonization, the country was populated gradually. First came African slaves, who were introduced in their thousands to build plantations. The average sugar plantation was made up of about four 800-yard sections, and stretched some 5½ miles inland. On these 7,500 acres of land would be no less than 40 miles of drainage channels and 140 miles of navigable canals for transportation and irrigation. According to the Venn Commission's enquiry into the sugar industry in 1948, 'the original construction

of these waterways must have entailed the moving of at least 100 million tons of soil. This meant that slaves moved 100 million tons of heavy, waterlogged clay with shovel in hand, while enduring conditions of perpetual mud and water.' It is hard to imagine what endurance, hardship and suffering must have been involved. The number of people who died during the construction of the waterways has not been documented, but certainly there were many. Their legacy is in the landscape, the literature of E.R. Braithwaite and Walter Rodney, among others, and essentially in the built environment.

Following the abolition of slavery in 1834, the population of Guyana was further swollen with the arrival of hundreds of thousands of indentured labourers from India, China and Portugal. With this fresh wave of immigrants came a period of vigorous social and cultural development. The government legislated to improve conditions for working people, and, with the pressure of increasing numbers, a building boom began. This lasted until the turn of the twentieth century.

GEORGETOWN: GARDEN CITY

In *Twenty-five Years in British Guiana* (1898), the Englishman Henry Kirke celebrates the architectural and natural landscape of Georgetown. It was widely praised as the garden city of the West Indies, and renowned for its charm and beauty, which came not only from its architecture but also from its layout, its trees and its gardens, as he explained:

Georgetown, the capital of British Guiana, the Venice of the West Indies, as it has been called, is certainly a strange place, and one calculated to excite the interest and admiration of every one ... the city is intersected in all directions by open canals and drains, which are crossed by innumerable bridges. These, at the time I first went out to the colony [in the early 1870s], were made of wood, which have since been replaced by handsome structures built of iron and cement. Main Street is certainly one of the prettiest streets I ever saw. About forty yards wide, it is divided up the middle by a wide canal full of the Victoria Regia lily, the canal, and the roads on each side, being shaded by an avenue of saman trees. Handsome houses, painted white, or some bright colour, are built on each side of the street, nearly all of [them] surrounded by gardens, full of crotons, palms, poinsettias, bougainvilleas, and all sorts of bright-hued plants and flowers; on some of the trees can be seen clusters of cattleyas [orchids] with their mauve and rose-coloured flowers; from another an oncidium [orchid] throws out its racemes of odorous petals, four to five feet in length. The Brick dam, as it is called, is another beautiful boulevard more than a mile in length, bordered on both sides by lovely flowering trees and lofty palms.

Houses in Guiana are almost entirely made of wood, raised upon brick pillars from eight to ten feet high, to enjoy the breeze, and avoid damp and malaria. The colony

provides excellent hardwood timber which will last for ages, but for cheapness builders, whilst using colony timber for the framework of the houses, use American lumber for the walls and partitions. This soon rots, the ants and the damp climate destroy it rapidly, and the outside of a house, despite frequent paintings, will require renewal every ten years. The system of drainage is primitive. The rain water is drained off by the canals, which are connected with the Demerara River by sluices …

… the excessive brightness of the place [is] caused by the width of the streets, the red roads, numerous fine white buildings and churches, the wealth of foliage and flower everywhere conspicuous, all lit up with an intense equatorial sunshine.

The city is embowered in trees: its aspect from the top of the lighthouse is of a sea of palms, out of which rise at intervals towers, spires, and campanile. For a great part of the year, the flamboyant trees make your eyes ache with the gorgeousness of their scarlet flowers, whilst in September and October the long-Johns break the sky line with their rich cream-coloured plumes, changing week by week to a real burnt sienna.

In 1973, in his autobiographical account *A Young Man's Journey*, the English botanist Nicholas Guppy described his first visit to Georgetown, when he was driven

into crowded streets of stilt-perched wooden houses, all painted white or gamboge [mustard-yellow], and all decorated with eaves, windows, roof-lines, doorways of frenzied, frilly fretwork. I glimpsed Stabroek market, a majestic late Victorian hulk whose writhings were in red-painted cast iron – it might have been in Brussels – soaring above piles of pineapples, mangoes, bananas, jostling vivid-coloured throngs of Negroes and Indians … we swung along the yellow and brown colonnaded front of the 1832 Greek revival government buildings, and out on to suddenly spacious streets. Two neatly-spired

early-nineteenth-century wooden gothic churches pointed primly among breadfruits and hibiscus – and we swept into what I always thought of as the 'zone of eccentricity' [where the] town hall, in the form of a weatherboard and cast-iron Rhenish castle, towered beside Baron Siccama's masterly law courts – an enormous rambling concrete and half-timbered Swiss chalet (1887), fronted by a dumpy statue of Queen Victoria, and [Arthur] Blomfield's Anglican Cathedral – the world's tallest, biggest and perhaps ugliest wooden building – in Puginesque Gothic …

Further still, double-landed streets broad as the Nevsky Prospect crossed at right angles on the grid plan laid out by the Dutch and French in the eighteenth century. Sometimes these streets still had Dutch-built canals running down their middles, but mostly these had been filled in, forming broad grassy or gravelled central avenues shady with saman trees … or flamboyants, cassias or jacarandas. Great barn-like wooden white-painted houses, like confections of snow, stood here amid enormous overflowing gardens. Mostly Georgian, Regency, or early Victorian in date, their classical details had been attenuated into needy elegance in the translation of stone or stucco into wood. 'Demerara Windows', vertically hung louvres pushed out from lacy fretwork sills by a pole, gave glimpses of cavernous interiors; while their 'wind-towers', enclosed spiral staircases with glassed-in summit rooms, designed for hot evenings or to watch ships go by on the river, rose above the tossing foliage …

… my hotel [was] in badly-done wooden Plantation-Romanesque style.

Here, Guppy conjures the mixed European influences on the architecture of Georgetown (a city of which he was not particularly fond), giving a sense of the incongruousness of the various colonial styles jostling and clashing. However, he also pinpoints lyrical elements that introduce harmony, giving a sense that individual creativity has had a hand in blending and

27

At first glance, this juxtaposition of elements appears to make up what in most cities would be a shanty town. On closer inspection, however, one can see shutters and sash windows that are still intact. The building on the left has external shutters over the sash window, for protection from the glare of the afternoon sun. The right-hand building retains its louvres and sash windows. A makeshift structure joins the two houses. Both buildings are elevated on short stilts, and the building on the right has an entrance porch and small balcony. It was a well-considered and well-constructed little cottage.

domesticating the different influences of local craftsmen, working in wood to give the colonial buildings a touch of originality. The political activist Rory Westmaas paid tribute to these local craftsmen and their work in his essay 'Building Under Our Sun' (1970), when he described 'fretwork panels over entrance doors, gallery window heads, spandrels in the angles of timber arches to the drawing rooms and on porches – interpretations in timber of cast-iron details'.

Both Guppy and Kirke describe the beauty and colour of the gardens around the buildings. Georgetown is structured in a grid, but a very spacious one, which allows breezes from the Atlantic Ocean to flow freely through and cool the city. In describing his experience of living and working in Georgetown, Guppy said that his office was in a 'small wooden building', 'where the sea wall met the Demerara River's mouth … When I looked out of its window there was no land between me and Africa, and the steady trade winds that buffeted us continuously were so insistent that every sheet of paper had to be held down with a weight … It was the coolest, pleasantest working place in the whole city.' The handsome architecture of Georgetown, painted white to look clean and bright, along with its grid layout of wide streets, avenues of large flowering trees and colourful domestic gardens, gave the city's inhabitants the sense of living in a beautiful, spacious, breezy garden, which created cooling shade from the sun and made it a pleasure to live in.

THE DEVELOPMENT OF THE COLONIAL HOUSE IN GEORGETOWN

The city of Georgetown was created through the amalgamation of a number of plantation holdings and the small villages lodged on them. These became known as wards. As the plantations came together, the city's population began to grow and so did its housing requirements. By the beginning of the nineteenth century the city comprised three wards: Stabroek, Werk-en-Rust and Robbstown-Newtown. In 1804 Stabroek, the oldest part of the city, was connected to the small village of Lacytown by bridges. The latter was incorporated into the city in 1852. Charlestown's boundaries were laid out in 1806 and extended in the 1820s, although most of the earlier town was destroyed by fire in 1828. Cummingsburg, one of Georgetown's oldest boroughs, and Kingston were both rebuilt after being destroyed by fire in the early nineteenth century. The rebuilding of these fire-damaged areas enhanced the expansion of the city in the second half of the nineteenth century, creating the boulevards, canals and buildings that we see in the twenty-first. Albert Town, Albouystown and Lodge were planned out in 1839, and building plots were sold to ex-slaves, or 'freedmen'. Indeed, Albouystown was constructed on the land of the sugar plantations in the 1860s. Both Wortmanville and Lodge districts were reclaimed from the plantations in the late nineteenth century, and grew rapidly until the turn of the twentieth century. In addition, the areas on the former plantation of Vlissengen were extended into Bourda and put into residential use during the 1880s. Although population growth was concentrated within the limits of the town, there was a great deal of development into what was then still plantation land.

The census register of 1851 shows that the suburbs Newburg-Freeburg, Albert Town and Wortmanville-Lodge contained nearly 5,000 inhabitants at that time, about 20 per cent of the population of the entire Georgetown area. The decision to build outside the wards may have

Above
In its heyday, this wonderful example of a grand old Georgetown house (photographed in 1998) would have been surrounded by other structures of similar stature in immaculately landscaped gardens. Unfortunately, all has now gone and the buildings on either side are of more recent date. This house in Queenstown has now been demolished.

Overleaf
Main Street was originally constructed as a canal, which fed water into the Lamaha Canal and then out to sea. In 1923 it was filled in and this avenue created.

been brought about by the lower cost of land there, the lower rate of taxation and the less strict (or in some cases absence of) building regulations outside recognized town boundaries. The disadvantages, however, were an increased risk of fire, a lack of mains water supply and inadequate lighting until the mid-twentieth century. More central, older parts of the city, such as Stabroek, Kingston and Cummingsburg, had enjoyed these facilities for many years.

It is worth reflecting here on the work of the nineteenth-century Welsh social reformer Robert Owen, one of a new breed of industrialists who created housing by building estates for their workers. He built factory towns, as did the Cadbury brothers, who provided similar housing for their workers in close proximity to their factories in England decades later. Following this model, plantation owners in the tropics built for their workers housing estates known as ranges. In his report 'Health Conditions of East Indian Employees on Sugar Estates' (1931), however, the English physician Sir Wilfred Beveridge called for a ban on the construction of ranges because of overcrowding and bad hygiene. Instead, he recommended that detached or semi-detached two-roomed cottages be built, which led the estates to comprise 986 cottages and 22 semi-detached buildings in total. As recently as the 1950s, the Booker brothers built social housing for workers on several plantations in Guyana, including the Blairmont Estate, southeast of Georgetown, and Bel Air Park in Kitty, Georgetown. In the 1970s the Guyana Trades Union Congress constructed similar buildings as part of its Tucville project in the south of the city, to house trades-union members.

By the mid-nineteenth century there was an established building industry in Georgetown, with a workforce skilled in the use of wood. Armed with plenty of raw material, these adept workers – their numbers inflated by indentured labour – were able to meet the demands of wealthy plantation owners and the need of the British for administrative offices and commercial buildings. In the resulting building boom, timber was the main construction material, although Dutch settlers had attempted to establish brick manufacturing in the eighteenth century.

Brickdam Church in the centre of Georgetown, constructed after a wooden church burned down, is a lasting reminder of their work. Dutch brick manufacturing was founded on the region's abundant supply of heavy clay, which was shaped and then dried in the sun. Brick was more widely used away from coastal areas, and although brick sluice supports, chimneys, forts and military installations still exist in the city, the material was rarely used in housing.

Fresh water was supplied to the city via the many springs and creeks that emerged on to the plain from the upper Demerara interior, and supplemented the fresh water acquired from artesian wells dug in the city. The earliest recorded artesian well was sunk in 1831 at Fort William Frederick, at the mouth of the river. By 1842 there were nine such wells working in tandem with the creek supply to the city. The Lamaha Canal – essentially a reservoir from which water was pumped – had been opened in 1825, and by 1880, with the addition of the artesian wells and other reservoirs, fresh water could be piped to most houses in the city. If there were several houses on a plot, as was often the case, a communal standpipe was used. From this buckets were filled and either stored in a cooler or left on the ledge of the Demerara window to remain chilled.

The Lamaha Canal extended from Waterloo Street in the west to Bel Air Park in the east of the city, and provided filtered water to the houses of Georgetown over a distance of approximately 6 miles. In 1922–23 the stretch from Vlissengen Road to Waterloo Street was filled in, and the pumping station moved to between Vlissengen Road and Sherriff Street, with the Botanic Gardens to the south. This new configuration effectively reduced the canal's storage capacity, but with the installation of new machinery, the plant offered greater pumping efficiency and was able to meet the demands of the expanding city.

A study of buildings in Georgetown cannot be complete without reference to the number of devastating fires that scarred the city. The first fire of note was in 1828 and destroyed most of Newtown and Charlestown. There were many smaller outbreaks before and after that, but the

Opposite
This well-maintained three-storey house in Queenstown has wide wooden awnings as well as the traditional Demerara windows.

Above
This derelict little cottage displays all the features that relate to the development of the Georgetown house. It is elevated on short, stubby stilts. The side addition, which would have contained the kitchen, is still just present, as are the windowsills and wall panels.

next significant blaze was in 1844, destroying most of High Street, South Road and Regent Street. These areas were totally rebuilt, only to be ravaged by fire again in 1864, as was Water Street. Fires were so frequent that in 1865 a local insurance firm, the Hand in Hand Insurance Co., was established to protect businesses that were considered at risk. The list of fires in Georgetown is seemingly endless, and many famous churches, residential buildings, cinemas, hotels and even whole city blocks were destroyed, with the loss of innumerable lives. The most recent devastating series of fires occurred in the mid-1960s, when most of downtown Georgetown was destroyed, including a number of wharf buildings along Water Street and the older parts of the city centre.

During the French occupation and until the 1830s (after the Great Charlestown Fire of 1828), and again during the British administration, fire regulations were gradually introduced as domestic fires became common. The regulations specified wider streets and, importantly, fixed plots without subdivisions and a minimum distance of 4 feet between buildings. Houses over 500 square feet in area were required to have brick kitchens, and dwelling houses had to be covered by slate, tiled or metal roofs. As a result, the densely built housing with its thatched roofs, constructed by unregulated builders, was brought under control. The subdivision of plots was not allowed until 1860. These fire regulations still exist – with amendments – but since the dwellings are much larger than envisaged, fire hazards remain.

The work of the English colonial architect Joseph Hadfield, who had built many of the larger public buildings in Georgetown during the 1830s, was distinctive in that it combined largely brick-built lower levels with timber upper parts and cement stucco, painted to resemble stone. Brick footings bore down on rafts of greenheart wood piled into the ground to sustain the increased load imposed by the brick. Some of Hadfield's buildings were constructed using cast-iron columns and metal railings, and embellished with painted wood pediments on the exterior and vaulted ceilings in the interior. These buildings provided the fashionable template for the wooden houses that are now commonplace.

Above
Camp Street (see pages 10–11).

Opposite
This building, set in its landscaped garden, is typical of the houses to be found in the residential ward of Queenstown. Its ground floor has been enclosed to provide extra accommodation, but an exterior staircase still leads up to the entrance.

Pages 36–37
Not for sale: a once very dilapidated building in Crown Street, Queenstown, undergoing major restoration.

ARCHITECTURAL STYLE

The buildings of Georgetown developed in clearly defined stages, but all followed the broad concept of the house on stilts. Since land was abundant, the original Dutch planners had divided residential areas into large plots, so there was little restriction on the size of houses, apart from the economics of building. As the English administrators and gentry settled into the colony, standards of living improved and the houses became bigger, a clear indication of the growing wealth of the colony and of the colonists and merchants who controlled it.

It was during the mid-nineteenth century that most of the great buildings were constructed and the architectural style of Guyana established. Paradoxically, this was also the time of great fires that destroyed many of the original buildings. Embellishments began to appear, such as the shady covered area known as the veranda, at front and back of buildings, its roof held up with light pillars, creating social space between the street and the interior of the house. The veranda also gave respite from the worst of the morning glare or afternoon sun, providing cool areas where people could meet or just sit and watch the world go by. Gradually, the front verandas were enclosed and later they disappeared altogether, creating a gallery at the front and back of the house. Today it is very rare to see an open veranda in Georgetown, but closer inspection of certain contemporary interiors reveals detailing that is usually reserved for facades that were once external.

The kitchen was housed in an outbuilding, with a wash-house between it and the main building. The middle of the main house accommodated living rooms and bedrooms, resulting in a longitudinal progression from the front gallery all the way to the kitchen and bathroom at the back.

In an attempt to reduce the amount of direct sunlight entering the house, the builder James Bradshaw Sharples (see page 108) had the idea of introducing stained-glass windows

Georgetown is littered with these small, abandoned and dilapidated cottages, which are gradually collapsing and vanishing – present only in these images, which attempt to capture them for posterity. All the common features are here: Demerara windows, glazed sash windows, jalousies, decorative fretwork and, in the image above, a kitchen extension added to the rear.

This house just off Carmichael Street in Cummingsburg possesses one of the rarest features of the Georgetown house inherited from the British tradition: the bay window on the left. The cantilevered porch allowing access to the garage below is another unusual feature of the building.

into his designs. This style became popular in the 1830s, and can be seen in a great variety of buildings in Georgetown, although few of the original structures have survived.

The veranda of the basic house plan was gradually enclosed to become a gallery, enabling the creation of a second bedroom on the upper floor. A dining room in part of the back gallery and a 'lean-to' kitchen and bathroom completed the common scheme that can still be seen today in the smaller dwellings of the city's less affluent wards. Subsequent changes have been more in terms of the detailing of the various parts, such as the ornamentation of the veranda. Each builder added his own fretwork pattern; the clover-leaf pattern, with variations interlocked with the circle, is one of a number of basic motifs incorporated into decorative fretwork.

The motifs on verandas became classic emblems of Guyanese architecture from the late nineteenth to the mid-twentieth century. Since the veranda and landing now served as an enclosure for privacy, so the stairs, which originally had a straight approach, were turned to the side to run parallel to the front of the house. Parallel stairs and landings were the standard approach to the first floor of the typical Guyanese house. On the first floor would be a covered landing with decorative motifs around its circumference and handrails. Since this part of the house was the most public, it was always the most ornate, with whitewashed fretwork and white columns.

Keeping the interior of a tropical house cool in the midday sun is always a problem for builders, but the Guyanese solved the problem with an arrangement of slats and louvres on the outside walls, known as jalousies. The spaces between the studs, usually on the upper floors, would be fitted with pine slats or louvres above or below a window or along a complete wall, allowing the free movement of air through the gallery while excluding rain and excessive sunlight. Whole parts of the external enclosure might be constructed in this way. During the 1950s many homes had this detail removed, in favour of solid panels. Often, where it was retained, it was adapted with mesh behind to prevent insect infestation. Early houses in

The Masons' Lodge on Carmichael Street is a very unusual building. It displays few of the architectural characteristics usually associated with buildings of the nineteenth century, when it was constructed – there are no Demerara windows, jalousies or first-floor gallery. However, it is still an elegant and well-proportioned wooden building on stilts.

Georgetown were built without glass. Glazing that is evident on older buildings would have been installed to replace the original jalousies or louvred windows.

Some modern houses (those built after 1945) are constructed with rigid slats angled downwards to provide a similar movement of air, but these cannot, strictly speaking, be termed jalousies. In these houses the double pitch of the porch roof projecting from the gallery creates a portico over the staircase, embellishing the central feature of the front elevation of the house. In large houses, a double stair was built to reinforce the classical symmetry.

The early kitchen, or more accurately the fireplace, was merely a raised platform or table structure with a roof and three sides to protect the pot and charcoal fire from wind and rain. As the house evolved, the kitchen developed in a similar way to the veranda, going through various stages of adaptation that bore a direct relationship to the expansion of the family and increasing affluence.

The first kitchens were timber additions at the back of the house. At sill height there would be a projection constructed of a more durable material, such as stone, concrete or compacted mud. On it was placed an oven or coal pot (a charcoal burner, the forerunner of the kitchen range). Later, during the 1880s, better homes would undoubtedly have had wood-burning stoves or AGA-type ranges. To stop the inevitable fires generated by the open charcoal apparatus, concrete platforms were constructed on a base of greenheart (a very hard timber that grows in straight poles and is used in the construction of buildings, wharves and harbours). The walls of the kitchen were vented to allow smoke out, while the surrounding walls were comprised of wood latticework to create good cross-ventilation while remaining in keeping with the aesthetics of the house. Cylindrical chimneys of beaten galvanized metal were attached to the stove and passed through the back of the kitchen and through the roof.

In the first half of the nineteenth century the main building was split into two rooms: the bedroom and the living room. This produced a new level of privacy in a now stable and emerging

Opposite
This simple cottage has traditional wooden louvred windows and decorative panelling below the sills. The glass windows are painted with whitewash, a practice commonly employed to reduce glare from the sun. The timber substructure is exposed, as are the clay-brick stilts on which the house sits.

Above
The interior of this large mansion in Kingston became visible as it was demolished in 2004. Boxes to contain weights for the sash mechanism are evident on either side of the window, as are the panelling, skirting boards and wooden structural details, including arches and fretwork.

domestic life. Sanitary areas were confined to outbuildings until the 1880s, when developments in Victorian engineering enabled lavatories to be brought inside. In fact, by the 1850s larger houses were connected to a limited sewage disposal system that pumped waste into the sea. Most houses, however, had a septic tank that had to be pumped out either by hand or with a petrol-driven pump mounted on a horse-drawn cart; the waste was then dumped in the sea. Before setting about this unpleasant task, the crew would light a series of fires with a pot on top containing a strong-smelling material such as the bark of the purpleheart tree to counteract the smell of sewage. Between 1922 and 1925 a comprehensive sewage network was built to serve what was then all of Georgetown, an area of some 5 square miles. No longer were citizens subjected to unbearable smells and dependent on Atlantic tides to clean their city.

The electric lighting of streets began in 1891. Limited street lighting had previously been provided by gas, but domestic gas lighting was limited owing to the fire risk. In that year alone fifty lamps were installed in the streets of Georgetown, while the Electric Lighting Company, which was established by Messrs Conrad, Allen and Turner in 1889, connected 650 dwellings.

The new lamps were mounted on tall poles of locally sourced greenheart, as opposed to the imported softer pine. However, large amounts of North American pine were used in the building industry at this time because it was found that the native timbers – all hardwoods – were too difficult for the intricate work that was demanded by clients and contractors. Hardwood also blunted tools very quickly, creating a growth industry of tool-sharpening. Indeed, as late as the 1950s travelling tool-sharpening artisans still commonly roamed the streets filing tools and knives on a hand-wound grinding stone transported by a horse or, more than likely, a 'donkey cart'.

One fine example of the use of pine is in the construction of the Demerara window, which has a sloping top-hung shutter that projects from the face of the building and can be opened outwards up to 2 feet by the use of a window stick. The triangular sides of the projection come

Above
Fretwork detailing and Georgian sash windows are the defining feature of the portico of the White Blossom Flower Lodge in Albert Town. The fretwork is made of the softer imported Canadian pine, unlike the main structure of the house, which is constructed from the harder, more robust native purpleheart or greenheart timber.

Opposite
Main Street is seen through the Demerara windows of the first-floor gallery of the Walter Roth Museum.

out at some 30 degrees and are always meticulously detailed with fine pine fretwork, allowing air to pass through the sides of the window when the shutter is down. The brackets supporting the sill project up to 18 inches. Rhythm is given to the facade by sash windows as well, or perhaps simple openings for ventilation and light.

Dutch brick columns were introduced in the early nineteenth century and were built to a height of 8–10 feet with a 15-inch square tapering at the top of one face, usually the outer. The major timber tie beams, measuring 8 by 12 inches or 6 by 10 inches, would rest on top of the column, and on this platform the upper house would be built. Such columns were originally constructed from bricks brought in as ballast in ships, but brickmaking later developed in Georgetown, as we have seen. An average single-storey house would have about twelve such columns placed at 19-foot intervals in runs of three, with a ring beam on top. The main joists were 4 feet apart, and on top of them boards of 8 by 1 inches were common. This use of brick columns and the method of construction were by no means universal, however: timber dimensions would be determined by the sawmills and tailored on-site by the builders.

The vacant area underneath the house was free to be used as stables, a play area, workshops or, perhaps more likely, servants' quarters. Today it is often used as a garage, utility room or games room. A valuable recreation space, it provided shelter from both sun and rain, and was also convenient for laundry.

The science and understanding of the builders during the period of wooden house construction in Guyana is yet to be surpassed. The modern concrete enclosed house, designed to accommodate air-conditioning and cooling electric fans, is vastly inferior in terms of design, layout, suitability to the local climate and aesthetics (air-conditioning units hanging out of buildings, with rust stains, are not a pretty sight), and also in environmental comfort.

HOUSES WITH TOWERS

Towers are quite common in the architectural landscape of Georgetown, and can be seen in any town of any size in the country. The buildings of which a tower forms a part take several forms, having been created as either single- or two-storey dwellings.

Towers – known locally as the Captain Towers of Kingston – are a good example of the evolution of a distinctive characteristic from the grand eighteenth-century dwelling into a regular architectural feature of Georgetown. The tall, slender tower is common in English, French and Italian architecture, and can be seen extensively in stone buildings found in the Urbino region of Italy. In Guyana the structure is built as an appendage on the front of the house and is displaced to one side. Entry to the ground floor is via an enclosed staircase that leads to the first floor. If space is confined, a dog-leg staircase is used; otherwise the stair is L-shaped. The first floor houses the study or family room, and there are two or three floors above. Those towers that house a complete staircase have louvres and jalousies at the top to direct draughts down towards the front door. The louvres are decorated with stained-glass windows to reduce glare. Outside is a railed catwalk or widow's walk.

The remainder of the house comprises a gallery, dining room, bathroom and rear kitchen on the first floor, and bedrooms on the upper floor, on the less sunny side. Thus the bedrooms have the advantage of being cool in the afternoon and evening, when the sun has passed overhead and is descending to the southwest. Most windows have coloured stained glass and louvres below jalousies and panelling. In some smaller tower houses the ground floor is partly enclosed by timber latticework painted white. Houses in other towns, such as New Amsterdam, have different, unique, orientations and generally shorter towers. One aspect of the tower house is the lack of any suggestion of a veranda on the exterior.

Some towers have living rooms, libraries and studies on the upper floors, while others contain the main staircase of the house, leading up to viewing platforms.

Above
This style of single-storey house, with its truncated tower containing the main stair, is fairly common in Georgetown. This particular building in Kingston appears to have been refurbished at some point, when the front gallery and stair tower were added – or perhaps the front staircase and gallery were enclosed, since they appear inconsistent with the rear part of the building.

Opposite
Many of the towers were constructed to give a good view over the city, towards the sea.

The fretwork detailing suggests that all the tower houses in Guyana were built within thirty years of one another. The buildings of W. Haley (after whom Haley Street was named), and H.O. Durham's tower house at Church and Camp streets (see page 140), substantiate this view. These buildings were said to have been commissioned by local ship-owners and merchants, and were used to observe the ships as they came into port.

THREE-STOREY HOUSES

This three-storey shingle house at Camp and Charlotte streets (above) is now the Christian Mission Church. The building shown opposite has a remarkably similar profile. The main body of each building is on three floors, with three sets of sash windows on two floors and a central gable-end window at the top. Both have an enclosed veranda on one side and an extension for the kitchen on the other. The church's shingle cladding suggests that it is the older of the two.

Old photographs of Georgetown show a profusion of three-storey buildings, of which few have survived the ravages of time and fire. These buildings, like the shingle-clad house (see page 59), are rapidly disappearing, and those that remain are costly to maintain and occupy valuable land in the city. Most were built by European merchants in the nineteenth and early twentieth centuries, and the best examples date from between 1880 and 1920. The upper floors of these houses are approached via an internal staircase in the southwest corner of the back gallery, away from the afternoon sun. The bedrooms are on the upper floors, possibly with an en suite bathroom. The first floor is free to be used as a living area with a dining room, drawing room and morning room facing west, away from the morning sun. There is also an office or a library, beyond which are the kitchen, pantry and back stairs. The open-gallery first floors, with their various functions, cover an area of as much as 800 square feet, creating a light and airy space. Tinted glazed panels are inserted in the outside walls of the staircases, giving a bright route to the upper floors.

These big houses are set back in wide landscaped grounds or on corners with flower gardens, lawns and fruit trees. They have the obligatory white paling fences of their time, with symmetrical or central gates and long drives. They are always orientated towards the sea, facing east to take advantage of the cooling coastal breezes and Atlantic Ocean sunrises. There are several examples of these houses in the Kingston area and on Main Street, Cummingsburg, that have been converted into embassies and government offices, some with commercial premises and shops on the ground floor. A number of other prestigious three-storey houses were built by the colonial governments of the time to house various government departments. Porticoes and pediments were common, as well as the finer detailing associated with nineteenth-century English Victorian architecture, but they were constructed by local builders. Unfortunately, poor maintenance, fire and general lack of use mean that few have survived.

A fine three-storey house on Main Street.

SHINGLE-CLAD HOUSES

The sight in Georgetown of a house clad in shingle is now rare. The buildings vary in size from a single bedroom unit with kitchen and bathroom, usually low (raised only about 4–5 feet off the ground), to the fairly substantial houses of the middle classes, which have up to four bedrooms and are built over two or three floors.

By the late nineteenth century, more than 60 per cent of Georgetown's housing was clad with wallaba bark shingles laid in rows like tiles pinned to batons. This outer layer insulated the interior of the dwelling from direct sunlight and heat. Maintaining this exterior cladding became increasingly difficult and costly, however, and in many cases it was removed altogether and the timber boards underneath painted. The practice of cladding new buildings in shingle was abandoned for economic reasons. The very few of these buildings that remain in Georgetown today are in a sorry state of repair.

Examples of the shingle-clad house in Waterloo and Camp streets. The shingle is made of dried wallaba bark, fixed to battens and painted.

Above
This once-beautiful front
porch has turned spindles
and fretwork eaves. The
replacement concrete block
columns are evidence of the
frailty of wooden construction in
a humid climate.

Opposite
This old house was the home
of the Order of Ancient Free
Gardeners, a fact that is
perhaps borne out by the lush
vegetation that surrounds it.

Above and opposite
An assortment of small town houses with intriguing details. Most retain their original shingle cladding, fixed wood louvres and glazed sash windows.

Right
A rare example of softwood decorative panels fixed to the exterior of a house. The original jalousie vents can be seen above, with the modern glass louvres that are now replacing them on most surviving buildings. The bottom beading of the decorative panel is missing, showing that remedial work was undertaken and the important bead not replaced afterwards.

Overleaf
Number 330 Church Street, at the junction of Church and Cummings streets in Queenstown, has a very large enclosed veranda, which creates a first-floor gallery with shuttered windows and louvred lower panels. The gallery encloses the house on the two street sides. The original Demerara windows are evident on the second floor, as is the decorative fretwork on the eaves of the roof and stair landing. The house, which dates from 1850, belonged to Abraham Isaacson, a pharmacist and rabbi. It is believed to have been used for Jewish worship in the absence of a synagogue in Georgetown.

THE WOODEN HOUSES
OF GEORGETOWN

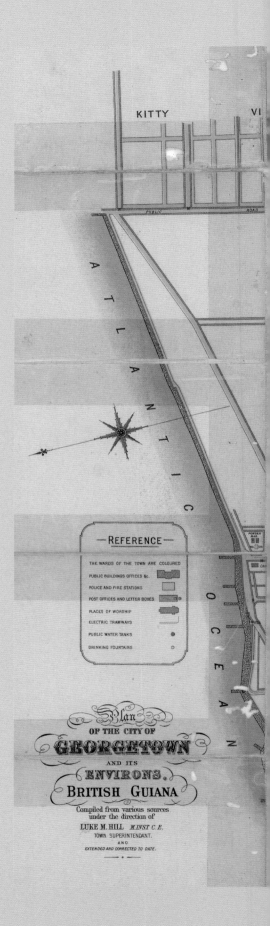

Of all Caribbean cities, none owes as much as Georgetown to the legacy of the nineteenth-century plantation system in terms of layout. The conversion of the fertile, waterlogged floodplain of the Demerara River into productive agricultural land during the eighteenth and nineteenth centuries defined the grid-type layout of the city's infrastructure as well as the style of its buildings.

Hundreds of miles of dams and canals criss-cross the Georgetown basin. The dams block the sea and the river, while the canals and trenches drain the enormous quantities of water produced by the region's prodigious rainfall. Towards the end of the nineteenth century the high dams developed into essential road connections: Vlissengen Road, High Street and the Back Dam. However, the essential contributor to the appearance of Georgetown is the profusion of drainage canals and reservoirs that penetrate the city and the many bridges that cross them – hence Henry Kirke's characterization of the city as the 'Venice of the West Indies'. The banks of the canals were planted with palms and other native trees to stabilize the soil and prevent erosion, and in the latter part of the twentieth century the canals were filled in to create the wide streets and avenues we see today.

The maps and descriptions that follow were assembled with the assistance of the National Trust of Guyana. The maps provide a clear outline of the linear nature of the plantations and the methodical way in which they were transformed from agricultural land into an English colonial city.

Plan of the City of Georgetown and its Environs, British Guiana, compiled from various sources under the direction of Luke M. Hill, Town Superintendent, nineteenth century, published by The Argosy.

66

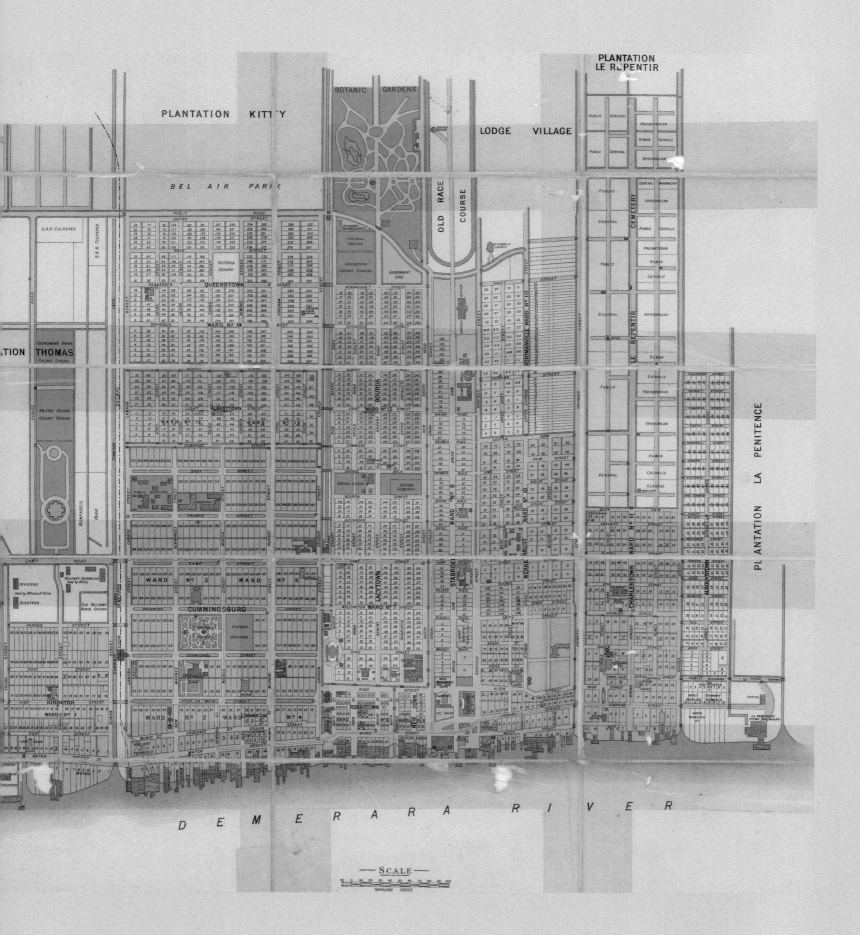

QUEENSTOWN

The ward of Queenstown had its birth as a plantation purchased by the Georgetown council in 1887 from Quintin Hogg, a planter and landowner. It was named in homage to Queen Victoria. Some of its streets were also given royal links, such as Albert Street, named after the queen's consort. Other streets commemorated local dignitaries: Peter Rose Street bears the name of a former member of the Court of Policy, while Forshaw Street was named after a mayor of the city, George Anderson Forshaw. Other streets were linked more directly to local topography: for example, Laluni and Anira streets were named after tributaries of the Lamaha, an offshoot of the Mahaica River.

Queenstown, as its name suggests, was an affluent area with wide streets and large wooden houses set in landscaped gardens. Most of this lush urban landscape has survived, as has the stock of large town houses standing on their own un-subdivided plots.

Right
The Queenstown Moravian Church, a unique Georgetown landmark, is a wooden building in the classic tradition. It was built in 1891, largely thanks to the initiative of the Reverend John Dingwall.

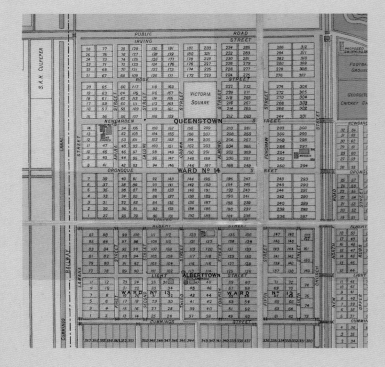

This page and opposite
An assortment of Queenstown's wooden houses. All are in a partially derelict state and in need of urgent care.

Overleaf
A very dilapidated house on Fifth Street, in need of some attention. The back addition of the kitchen can be clearly seen to the left, as can the front addition of the veranda, which was enclosed to create the gallery to the extreme right.

CASTELLANI HOUSE
VLISSENGEN ROAD QUEENSTOWN

One of the most admired, documented and photographed buildings in Georgetown is Castellani House, a unique building named after its creator, Cesar Castellani. The building stands in a prominent position beside the botanical gardens at the junction of Vlissengen Road and Homestretch Avenue. It was constructed between 1879 and 1882 as a residence for the city's chief botanist, George Jenman, who was appointed to oversee the development of the fledgling botanical gardens. The house was later used by successive government agricultural departments, until 1965, when it became the residence of the prime minister and subsequently president Linden Forbes Burnham, until his death in 1985. It is now the home of the National Art Collection, and was officially named Castellani House in 1993.

Cesar Castellani

The architect Cesar Castellani was born in Malta and arrived in British Guiana in 1860 in the company of a group of Italian priests. It is not known whether he was trained in architecture, but his skill in the design and construction of buildings in the local materials available to him was prodigious. He constructed numerous buildings in Georgetown, among them Brickdam Cathedral, probably one of the largest stone buildings in the city at the time; Brickdam Police Station; New Amsterdam Hospital; and parts of the Church of the Sacred Heart. In 1875 Castellani was commissioned to design the ceilings of the new Parliamentary chamber. His name has also been linked to the building of the Victoria Law Court, which was previously credited to Baron Hora Siccama, the architect of several state buildings in Georgetown.

On the front facade of
St Stanislaus College on
Brickdam, designed by
Castellani, cast-iron 'fretwork'
forms the capitals of columns
that imitate the timber detailing
of local houses.

The massing of St Stanislaus
College is on a larger scale
than that of most houses in
Georgetown, but the design
and detailing take several cues
from the colonial domestic
architecture.

This assortment of buildings in Queenstown reflects various styles and construction methods, from the concrete of the 1960s and the zinc awnings of the 1950s (this page) to the much older colonial town houses, some of them in ornate gardens (opposite).

A well-maintained town house in Queenstown, set in a large, lush garden. This building has the elongated profile typical of houses built on wide but shallow plots.

THE BRAZILIAN AMBASSADOR'S RESIDENCE
ANIRA AND PETER ROSE STREETS
QUEENSTOWN

On the corner of Anira and Peter Rose streets stands a spectacular building, now sensitively restored, which has been the residence of the Brazilian Ambassador since the 1970s. It was commissioned by the De Freitas brothers and, surprisingly, constructed as late as 1939–40, yet it displays all the classic detailing of a nineteenth-century building, such as decorative fretwork, spindles and Demerara windows. The house retains its open veranda, and has an elaborately decorated front double-return stair and landing.

This building on Brickdam is set in spacious grounds. The two-storey core of the house is unusually small in comparison to the enclosed veranda that surrounds it. The ground-floor stilts are also quite short, giving the building a singular profile.

Two modern buildings on Anira
Street, Queenstown.

KINGSTON

Kingston will always be associated with the plantation owner Cornelius Leary, who in 1759 was granted land to cultivate cotton and coffee near the mouth of the Demerara River. After his death his wife, Eve, inherited the estate. In 1796 a British garrison was established on what subsequently became known as the Eve Leary estate. At that time the town consisted of a number of small cottages set amid gardens; it later became known as Kingston.

This settlement at the confluence of the Demerara River and the Atlantic Ocean became a very salubrious place to live after Queenstown and Cummingsburg were established as residential areas in the early nineteenth century. Its attraction was its cool microclimate and its proximity to the port, making it particularly convenient for the merchant classes. Camp Street, which runs through Cummingsburg (see page 114) to Kingston, takes its name from the garrison to which it led. Other road names, such as Parade Street and Fort Street, relate to the area's military heritage; Duke Street was named after a son of King George III.

Right
The elegant Demerara windows of this large two-storey building in Kingston appear to be in the older part of the house, but in fact the rear addition is clad in wallaba shingle, an older material. To the extreme right is the more recent addition, the gallery, enclosed with louvres, vents and jalousies.

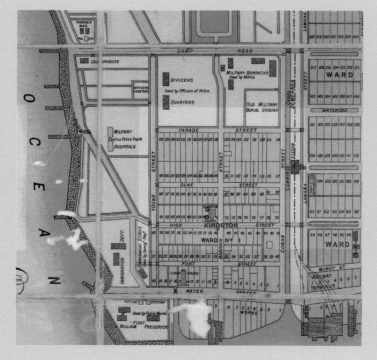

CANADIAN HIGH COMMISSION
YOUNG STREET
KINGSTON

This complex of gracious buildings is one of the jewels in the crown of Georgetown's architectural heritage. Thankfully, that fact has been recognized by its occupant, the Canadian High Commission, which acquired it in 1977 and has maintained the building with great care.

The house was home to the Sisters of Mercy in Guyana between 1949 and 1977, and still boasts ecclesiastical details, such as stained-glass windows. In addition, the building has all the elements of the classic nineteenth-century Georgetown house, including Demerara windows, panelled louvres and an unusual skylight. Its setting is very picturesque, at the junction of Main and Young streets; the latter is the last residential street in Kingston facing the Atlantic Ocean.

RED HOUSE
HIGH STREET
KINGSTON

The former home of Sir Eustace Woolford, Speaker of the House of Assembly, was acquired by the colony of British Guiana in 1925 and became the residence of British colonial secretaries until 1953. Its most recent resident was Dr Cheddi Jagan, who lived there as Premier of British Guiana between 1961 and 1964. In subsequent years the building housed government offices and the Public Service Ministry; it is now home to the Cheddi Jagan Research Centre and archive.

The date of this building is not known, but what is certain is that the structure we see today is not how it would have first looked. In fact, it may not even have been this colour. There have been various additions over the years, including a ground floor and an open veranda with an external staircase at the rear. The original tower remains, as does the wallaba shingle, now distinctively painted red.

ST JOSEPH MERCY HOSPITAL
PARADE STREET
KINGSTON

The St Joseph Mercy Hospital is one of the best-known and most recognizable buildings in Georgetown. Although it is not strictly a house, it is included in this book because it originated as a residential dwelling. The main body of the building is the original house, to which were added symmetrical extensions on either side in the 1940s. Its first incarnation after its renovation was as a nursing home, then the Sisters of Mercy had the building renovated to function as a hospital, which opened in 1945. Fortunately the renovation retained many of the building's original features.

ST JOSEPH MERCY HOSPITAL

The main Mercy Hospital building has been converted and developed over many years, but it retains its classic Demerara windows on the second floor and its enclosed veranda on the first floor, enhanced by a band of glazed jalousies. Unfortunately the building pictured on page 101, which was central to the Mercy Hospital Complex, was destroyed by fire in May 2010.

**ST JOSEPH MERCY
HOSPITAL**

The entrance to the physiotherapy department of the Mercy Hospital, as seen from Parade Street before and after renovations were carried out in about 2010. The building now has a grand entrance with a portico and a first-floor balcony.

AUSTIN HOUSE
HIGH STREET
KINGSTON

The first Kingston House was constructed in the early 1840s and demolished in 1894, when this building replaced it. It was renamed Austin House in 1921 in recognition of its early occupant, the first Anglican bishop of Guyana, William Piercy Austin, who had lived on the site from 1842 until his death in 1892. The building is still the residence of the bishops. Located at the corner of Barrack and High streets, the house has changed little since it was built in the late nineteenth century. A limited amount of construction on the ground floor to create space for offices was undertaken in the 1930s, but otherwise the building has remained true to its original style and form. It is yet another classic Georgetown 'big house', built on a grand scale and set in a mature garden filled with exotic palms and many indigenous trees and plants.

There are steep roofs with panelled Demerara windows on the second floor, coming down to six-panelled Georgian windows on the first floor. Many of the original details are still in place, such as the Canadian pine exterior walls and pine floors, with hitching posts for buggies, and cobbles under the house that would have been open to the elements. The original stained-glass windows are still in place, admitting a serene, diffused light to the bishop's private chapel.

AUSTIN HOUSE

Opposite
Austin House before its
renovation in 2012. The second-
floor Demerara windows and
the Georgian sash windows
on the first floor are clearly
visible. Unfortunately, since the
photograph was taken the lush
landscaped gardens have been
removed.

This page
The renovation in progress.

SHARPLES HOUSE
DUKE STREET
KINGSTON

The residential buildings of James Bradshaw Sharples (1799–1859) and his son John Bradshaw Sharples (1845–1913) greatly influenced the style of colonial domestic building in mid-nineteenth-century British Guiana. They displayed a level of sophistication and craftsmanship not expressed by many of their contemporaries.

In 1880 John Sharples established the British Guiana Sawmill and the Kingston Steam Woodworking Factory in Water Street, Kingston. These businesses were the foundation of his building projects, and he had a plentiful supply of raw materials and craftsmen at his disposal to bring his designs to fruition. From these premises he built all the railway stations, bridges and storage sheds on the Georgetown to New Amsterdam railway and the Rosignol railway line. Unfortunately, no physical evidence remains of these structures, although a number of Sharples's domestic buildings survive: among them one on the corner of Anira and Oronoque streets; 278 Forshaw Street in Queenstown; and this one, 92 Duke Street, Kingston. Others are still being discovered. The Bishop's House on Main Street in Kingston, now the Walter Roth Museum, has been credited to him (see page 116).

The family workshops, with the latest lathe and jigsaw machinery, were well equipped to produce the turned balustrades and high-quality fretwork seen on Sharples's balconies, Demerara windows and overhanging eaves. With the use of routers, Sharples was able to extend his design ideas to include the sculpting of faces on his doors, a feature evident in the Forshaw Street house.

These buildings also incorporated an abundance of wrought ironwork, a material rarely used in domestic building at the time. It brought delicacy to the facade and broke up the rhythm of the horizontal and vertical lines created by the jalousies and Demerara windows. The cast-iron balconies, stair columns and roof ridges are still evident on the Duke Street and Forshaw Street houses.

The surviving Sharples houses are easily recognized by their classic elements and by the detailed carvings of animals and figures on their wooden friezes and panels.

The photograph opposite shows the addition of a portico on the first floor of the Duke Street Sharples house. It was taken in 2015; the portico was added in about 2011.

OTHER SHARPLES HOUSES

A Sharples house on the corner
of Anira and Oronoque streets,
Queenstown.

This page
Forshaw Street, Queenstown.

A view from across the Lamaha Canal, from Laman Street to Cowan Street.

CUMMINGSBURG

In 1759 some 500 acres of land were granted to Jacques Salignac for the cultivation of coffee and cotton, and he named this tract of land La Bourgade. However, in 1807 Thomas Cumming, a Scotsman, acquired the estate and renamed the plantation Cummingsburg. It consisted of a town and estate 2 miles in circumference. He later donated the Promenade Gardens and Militia Parade Ground to the city.

A special feature of Cummingsburg was the provision of freshwater reservoirs, which were filled with small fish and later planted with the giant water lily *Victoria amazonica* (formerly *Victoria regia*) and lotuses (*Nelumbo*). The reservoir was filled in and converted into a walkway in 1897, renamed Victoria Promenade in recognition of the Queen's Diamond Jubilee that year. This area is now known as Main Street. In later years other reservoirs were converted into similar walkways. Water Street was formed by the original riverside dam, while Camp Street was the road that led to the garrison north of the city. In 1864 the western part of Cummingsburg was destroyed by fire. The subsequent creation of new streets and redistribution of house plots formed the layout we see today.

An examination of this ward of the city gives indications of Guyana's rich history. For instance, Waterloo Street was named after the Duke of Wellington's great battle against and victory over French forces on 18 June 1815, and Carmichael Street was named after General Hugh Lyle Carmichael, who served as governor of Demerara from 1812 until his death the following year. Quamina Street (formerly Murray Street, after Major General John Murray) was renamed in honour of one of Guyana's national heroes. Other streets derived their names simply from their geographic proximity to buildings or places; for example, Thomas Street was the main road to Plantation Thomas.

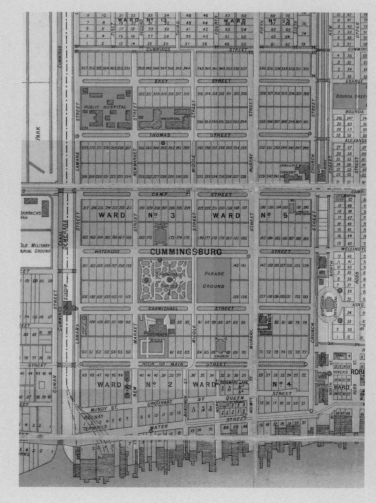

Although close to its neighbour on one side, this small house has a relatively large plot with a pleasant garden. The blue woodwork is a cheerful change from Georgetown's usual white.

115

WALTER ROTH MUSEUM
MAIN STREET
CUMMINGSBURG

The Walter Roth Museum is named after one of Cummingsburg's prominent occupants, an English physician and geologist who came to Guyana in 1907. Roth's predecessor in the house was one Duncan Hutson, an eminent barrister and legislator. As magistrate and protector of the Amerindians, Roth undertook much pioneering anthropological and archaeological research into Amerindian life in the colony. The museum was set up in 1980 as a permanent public exhibition dedicated to indigenous peoples, with the aim of reflecting their lives and folklore through an extensive collection of artefacts and relics assembled by Roth.

This well-proportioned house is attributed to John Sharples, and is thought to date from 1890. There is an inspiring amount of detail on its first-floor facade, with a rhythmic assembly of alternating glazed and Demerara shutters, terminating at one end in a stair tower. There may well have been stained glass on the top floor of the tower, interspersed with Demerara windows. The ground floor would have been enclosed to extend the living spaces when the house was used as a private residence.

The building was sold to the British government in 1942, and has had several occupants and uses since, including a teacher-training college and the Attorney General's Chambers (until 1980). It was later acquired by the National Trust, and in 2002 was restored by Guyana's Ministry of Culture, which continues to oversee its maintenance.

WALTER ROTH MUSEUM

Demerara windows seen from inside the Walter Roth Museum, looking out on to Main Street. These windows, with their open slats, elaborate fretwork vents and slatted louvres, allow air to pass freely through the building, dispensing with the need for mechanical cooling. The arrangement of windows and shutters gives a pleasing rhythm to the facade (see previous page).

THE PRIME MINISTER'S RESIDENCE
MAIN STREET
CUMMINGSBURG

The residence of the prime minister is a fine example of mid-nineteenth-century Georgetown architecture, with its central 'widow's walk' tower and unusual square cupola. An elegant, well-proportioned building with Italianate features, it has lofty ceilings, spacious rooms and decorative cornices, with Georgian-style twelve-pane sash windows that create an unusual balance with the local Demerara windows.

This impressive building was constructed for a Mr Sandbach and subsequently acquired by the Booker brothers, owners of Bookers Ltd. The Booker family sold it to the British government in 1962 to be used as the home of the British High Commission, and in 1987 the house was designated the official residence of the prime minster of Guyana.

THE PRIME MINISTER'S RESIDENCE

Of note inside the prime minister's residence are the cast-iron columns and the plasterwork on ceilings and walls. This building has been refurbished many times, but the integrity of its internal decoration has been preserved.

STATE HOUSE
MAIN STREET
CUMMINGSBURG

The official residence of the president of Guyana was formally known as Government House. Constructed in 1854, it was the home of the governors of British Guiana until 1966, when the first Guyanese governor general, Sir David Rose, took up residence. The building sits in a landscaped garden and occupies almost half a city block, with an entrance in Main Street and a secondary entrance in Carmichael Street. Of all the remaining great houses of Georgetown, it is particularly well placed for the holding of government functions.

State House at first appears to be a grand and inspiring piece of colonial architecture, but closer inspection reveals a number of uninspiring additions and extensions that create an imbalance about the facade, such as its air-conditioning units. However, the interior is well decorated, with carved panels and Georgian detailing of great elaboration to grace such a grand and important house.

GEORGETOWN CLUB
CAMP STREET
CUMMINGSBURG

This grand building became the home of the exclusive Georgetown Club in 1945, after the previous house on the site was destroyed by fire. Most of what we see today is the product of good restoration and attention to the classic roots of Guyanese architecture. The building has a fine gallery and ballroom, as befits one of the principal meeting places of Georgetown's social elite.

COLGRAIN HOUSE
CAMP STREET
CUMMINGSBURG

Colgrain House was reputedly named after the Scottish estate of its former owner, the Campbell family. It is now the official residence of the secretary general of the Caribbean Community (CARICOM). The son of Bishop William Austin, William George Gardner Austin, lived there in the 1890s. Other former proprietors included Bookers Ltd, which called it Booker House, and the Federal Republic of Germany, for which the house served as a residence until 1975, when it became the property of the Guyanese government.

This fine example of a classic Georgetown mansion house was built in the late nineteenth century. The building has been well preserved: its brick stilts are still evident and the ground floor has not suffered the indignity of having its sides filled in. The upper three storeys still display their Demerara windows, jalousies and slatted wood panelling. Under the eaves is a unique Georgian three-panelled window with a sunrise fanlight.

CARA LODGE
QUAMINA STREET
CUMMINGSBURG

Cara Lodge is presently a hotel, but was formerly one of the great houses of Georgetown's aristocrats, and has an illustrious history. It was constructed in the 1840s by a still unknown architect as two houses, the rear one being used as servants' quarters.

The house has had a number of influential owners and renowned guests. It was originally built for the Meservey family, and then passed to George Anderson Forshaw, mayor of Georgetown. He was visited in 1920 by Edward, Prince of Wales, who is said to have planted the sapodilla tree in the garden. In the 1950s the house's new owners, the Taitt family, made it the centre of Guyanese and Caribbean cultural life, and were visited by many artistic and literary figures of the time, including the artists Philip Moore and Ron Savory and the poet and playwright Derek Walcott. During the 1950s and 1960s the building was known as the Woodbine Club, and in 1982 it became the home of the Dorothy Taitt Foundation. The building, on the west side of Quamina Street, makes good use of its double-aspect plan.

Pages 132–33
Main Street, with its central shaded pedestrian avenue, runs from Kingston into the heart of Georgetown, and is one of the best-known streets in Georgetown. Until 1923 it was a canal that drained into the Lamaha Canal.

It is flanked by notable buildings, including the Walter Roth Museum, the Prime Minister's residence and the State House, and was once home to the United States Embassy. The Sacred Heart Cathedral is also here. At the junction with Church Street stands the Georgetown Cenotaph, terminating its axis. The Tower Hotel and the Georgetown Library are also at this junction, as was the famous Bookers department store, once a bastion of Georgetown city life.

MORAY HOUSE
CAMP AND QUAMINA STREETS
CUMMINGSBURG

Moray House is at the corner of Camp and Quamina streets, facing east, with its main entrance in Quamina Street. This side of the house is subjected to the full glare of the morning sun, so is well protected by an array of Demerara windows, as is the Camp Street facade. One of the unique features of this house is the enclosed rooftop gallery, with its blend of shutters and Demerara windows. The principal rooms and Demerara windows face east on to Quamina Street. The building is well designed to take advantage of its orientation.

Moray House was home to the De Caries family for many generations. In 2011 the Moray House Trust was set up in memory of the late David De Caries, who was instrumental in the foundation of the *Stabroek News*, still a very influential local newspaper. The building is now used for public lectures and exhibitions.

THE NATIONAL TRUST BUILDING

CARMICHAEL STREET
CUMMINGSBURG

It is fitting that the government body entrusted with the preservation and conservation of Guyana's historic buildings should occupy such a magnificent example of the Georgetown town house. This building sits proudly next to the State House and Georgetown Club (see pages 124 and 126) in Carmichael Street. It is a classic old building that has, among other vernacular features, a three-storey tower, which houses offices. It is adorned with its original Demerara windows and has a front first-floor enclosed gallery with a combination of jalousies and sash windows.

The Promenade Gardens, opposite the National Trust Building, were once part of a larger enclosure that included the Parade Ground (1812). They were originally developed in 1884 as an ornamental Victorian garden for the adjacent Government House (now State House). The two large open spaces have been separate since 1966, and the old Parade Ground is now known as Independence Park.

The Astor Cinema, on
Waterloo and Church streets,
Cummingsburg – although not
constructed as a dwelling – is a
landmark of central Georgetown. It
was closed in June 2013 and, like
many fine wooden buildings of its
ilk, has become dilapidated; it will
inevitably be destroyed.

This dilapidated house stood on the corner of Carmichael and Middle streets. It had a classic enclosed veranda and decorated porch, as well as a rear kitchen addition and an outhouse to the left. The original central body of the house is identifiable by the change in construction and roof line, and by the misalignment of panels on either side. The building was demolished not long after this photograph was taken.

TOWER HOUSE
CAMP AND CHURCH
STREETS
CUMMINGSBURG

Here, on the corner of
Camp and Church streets,
sits a very good example
of the tower house. It was
designed by H.O. Durham
and constructed in about
1924, originally as a two-
storey dwelling (the third
level was added later). The
tower, with its widow's walk,
is in the centre of the Church
Street facade. Along the
Camp Street facade, the
house has an array of sash
windows and decorative rails
with louvred windows on the
second storey and Demerara
shutters on the top floor. It
would have been built on
stilts, but today much of the
ground floor has been filled
in to create habitable rooms.

The house was originally
owned by the Kidman family
and was subsequently
bought by the popular
cricketer John A. Browne in
1937. In 1945 one Frederick
Kerry bought the house,
and in 1974 a Neville King
acquired it; he sold it in
1979 to the Guyanese
government. The building is
now home to the Go Invest
Organization.

In addition to the well-preserved
tower and wrought-iron balcony,
this building also has a bay
window on the first floor (right,
top). This bay is reflected on the
opposite side of the building (right,
bottom).

STABROEK

Georgetown's oldest ward is Stabroek, a rectangle ¼ mile wide and 1 mile long. It was established in 1782 by the Dutch West India Company and in 1784 named after Nicolaas Geelvinck, Lord of Stabroek, then president of the company. It was the first established settlement at the mouth of the Demerara River, and grew by merging with other towns that collectively became known as Georgetown.

Many of Stabroek's streets were named after prominent members of society, reflecting the prestigious nature of this ward. Several of the short streets running north to south were known by numbers before being amended by the mayor and town council in 1901. The ward's main thoroughfare, Croal Street, was named after John Croal, a mayor of Georgetown, but it was also known as Red Dam. It was paved with bricks and covered with burnt earth until 1921, when it was tarred over for the visit of the then Prince of Wales, later King Edward VII. Hadfield Street was named after Joseph Hadfield, an architect and former Crown Surveyor of the colony of British Guiana, and one of the more influential architects to have worked in Georgetown.

Previous pages
Among the houses shown here is one of very few bay windows in Georgetown (page 143, top). The bay obviously has its roots in Victorian architecture, but the central entrance and awning appear to be a very Guyanese invention.

Far right
This cottage in Stabroek has a striking bougainvillea and white picket fence. The remains of whitewash shading can be seen on the glass of the windows.

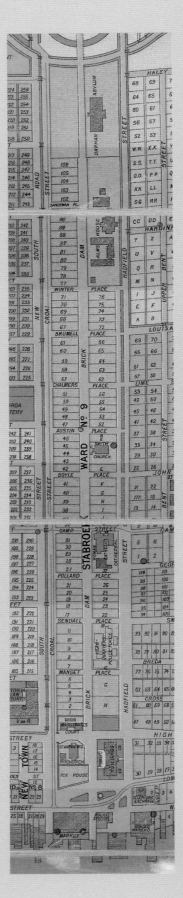

DEMICO HOUSE
LOMBARD STREET
STABROEK MARKET

Demico House stands on the corner of Lombard Street and Brickdam, facing Stabroek Market. It was not constructed as a residential building, but more as a place of entertainment and a hotel. The building is said to date from 1882. Although little is known about who designed it, we do know that it was sold in 1893 by Messrs Birch and Company to the D'Aguiar brothers, who named it the Demerara Ice House (DIH) and renovated it to incorporate a soft-drinks plant, a hotel and a bar. The building was notable for its very grand bar, which was said to have been designed by Cesar Castellani in 1896, although this cannot be verified. Unfortunately, the interior – apparently his answer to the cafés found in Paris and Berlin – was stripped out in the 1940s. The external metalwork and central clerestory on the upper floor are unique features of this building, designed to allow the free passage of light and air into the deep square plan of the building's interior.

Left
A house of classic simplicity on Brickdam, set in a landscaped garden.

Below
'Jack's', a unique building on Princess Street, Charlestown, may be modern, but it is bold in colour and classic in stature. It is constructed from concrete, yet manages to retain signs of its heritage, including its roofline, the arrangement of windows and even its position on the plot.

These three buildings at the junction of Middle and Camp streets illustrate very clearly the density and proximity of large wooden buildings. Many of the city's colonial wooden buildings have been lost through fire, notably that of 23 February 1945, and in 1963 as a result of political unrest. These fires destroyed most of the commercial sector of central Georgetown and Water Street.

ROBBSTOWN AND BOURDA

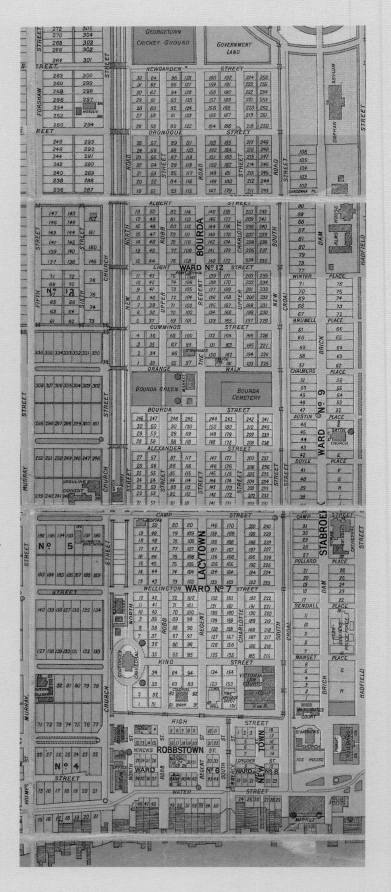

Joseph Bourda leased this plantation from the Crown in 1792, and subsequently sublet the property to John Robb, who arranged for it to be subdivided into building plots and lent his name to this area and to Robb Street. Bourda later gave his name to the adjacent ward of Bourda (see below). In 1864 the entire old town of Robbstown was destroyed by fire. Under the guidance of Mayor Edward John Barr, it was rebuilt with enlarged plots and wider streets, resulting in the present layout of the ward.

Joseph Bourda purchased the area that now bears his name to develop an estate as an offshoot of his Vlissengen plantation. In 1876 the ward was reorganized by the Vlissengen Commissioners, who were appointed by the government of British Guiana to investigate the cases of the many claimants to Bourda's estate. This very central ward contains the world-famous Bourda Market and the spectacular Bourda Cricket Ground. South Road, originally a footpath, is the southernmost street of the district.

In Robbstown and Bourda, as in many other parts of the city, streets were named after prominent members of society. Hinck Street in Robbstown, for example, is named after the politician Sir Francis Hincks, governor of British Guiana 1862–68 and later finance minister of Canada. In Bourda, Charlotte Street is named after Queen Charlotte, wife of King George III; Alexander Street for the tzar of Russia, Alexander I; Wellington Street after the Duke of Wellington; and King Street for George III himself.

Opposite
This house, between High Street and Smythe Street in Newburg, is one of few in Georgetown to have a bay window.

This social housing on Brickdam
– perhaps one of the last
such projects in the city – was
constructed in the 1950s and,
unusually for the times, made
from wood. Its layout is traditional,
with long terraces of dwellings that
share facilities.

This primary school on the corner of St Stephen and Princess streets, with its enclosed ground floor, moves away from the city's traditional building style. The author attended the nursery attached to this school, aged four.

DARGAN HOUSE
ROBB AND ORONOQUE STREETS BOURDA

At the corner of Robb and Oronoque streets in Bourda, Dargan House is a remarkably well-preserved icon of old Georgetown architecture. Not much is known of its builders or designers, but the house is a standard classic mansion with the distinction – as with Austin House in Kingston (see page 105) – of being one of the few buildings in the city to be named after its occupant. Patrick Dargan was a lawyer and legislator during the 1880s, campaigning for the poor and defending their rights against the established plutocracy of the time. The building now belongs to the government of Guyana and houses the UNESCO secretariat, among other national institutions.

Below
This building in the downtown area of Bourda is typical of the 1940s and 1950s, when traditional detailing was still being used but there was more glass on the front facade. The metal curved awning was developed, and is fairly common on buildings of the era.

Below
This former school was
constructed after the turn of the
new millennium, on Brickdam.
The architects have sensitively
incorporated the aesthetic of the
local architecture, resulting in
a balanced building.

Opposite
A house on Princess Street.

This unique house, on Irving Street, Queenstown, has its wooden frame on the outside, similar to English dwellings of the Tudor period. This method of construction was also used for the High Court (see page 20). The house has a hipped roof in the Dutch tradition, Demerara windows and a curved metal canopy on the ground floor. After this photograph was taken, in 2005, the building fell into disrepair and was demolished.

This building, part of a complex known affectionately throughout Georgetown as 'The Palms' (after the lush trees that lined upper Brickdam in the 1950s), was an almshouse that opened in 1874. It is said to have been designed by Cesar Castellani (see page 75), and in its day it was one of the grandest wooden buildings in Georgetown. It was very dilapidated when this photograph was taken, in 1996, and has since been demolished.

This substantial building stands on New Garden Street, opposite Georgetown Cricket Ground. It has casement windows and an iron staircase.

This exceptionally large town house is at the junction of Albert and Regent streets. Such an unfortunate position in a dense commercial area might well have led to its demise, but it retains all its second-floor Demerara windows and its glazed box sash windows on the first floor. It has a veranda on the left, facing Regent Street, and the little portico on the right would have sheltered the original back stairs.

Schoolchildren wait for their bus on the bridge at the junction of Croal and Camp streets. In the background of this tranquil scene is a well-preserved Georgetown town house.

The roof profile of this very large wooden building at the edge of colourful, bustling Bourda Market suggests that it was constructed in the fashion of the mid-1970s. However, in this photograph it appears incomplete, lying abandoned amid the market stalls. The building was demolished in 2015.

Left and pages 166–67
Such juxtapositions of old and new exemplify the tension between old Georgetown and the influence of Modernism. The picture on the left was taken in 2011; the wooden town house was later demolished and replaced with a concrete building of questionable quality.

Below
On Camp Street in 2010, the old also makes way for the new. The remains of a demolished wooden town house still litter the building site as the new concrete structure is erected.

The face of a changing city: new multistorey concrete structures can be found in many parts of Georgetown, replacing dilapidated wooden structures.

Opposite
An assortment of concrete buildings found around Georgetown and dating from the late 1950s to the present day. The earlier buildings would have been less reliant on mechanical ventilation, and incorporated various design techniques to avoid heat gain through the glazing. The windows are set back from the face of the building and at an angle to avoid direct sunlight. Most of these buildings had flat roofs, but extended roofs and balconies compensated for the loss of shade from wooden eaves.

This page
More recent concrete buildings ignore the environmental limitations of direct sunlight and heavy rainfall on the structure, and rely on mechanical means to function. In doing so, they lose the aesthetic and practical benefits of a 150-year history of architecture that evolved to blend with and accommodate its environment.

This new concrete building in Kingston sits very elegantly on stilts in a contemporary interpretation of the classic tradition. It has an open second-floor veranda and louvred windows on the left facade. On the first floor can be seen a sunscreen that resembles a Demerara window. It is altogether well composed and in harmony with its site.

This sensitively designed timber building at the junction of Thomas and Lamaha streets was constructed in the 1950s and is clearly representative of its era. Its front elevation, for example, has the traditional Demerara windows and veranda, but this facade is not over-ornamental and has minimal fretwork. Hanging baskets of orchids and ferns were a decorative feature of many houses in the 1950s and 1960s, and here they reflect the age of the house.

Right
This substantial house has been taken over by a department of the Guyanese government, as the flag shows.

Below
Herdmanston Lodge, at Peter Rose and Anira streets, Queenstown.

Opposite
A town house with a bay window in Newburg. This building is in poor condition and partly derelict. The porch and front staircase are about to collapse, as are the windows and bay. It is set in a very large plot and would lend itself to an inspired development project.

Dilapidated wooden houses on Princess Street, as seen from across the 'trench'.

CONCLUSION

The architecture of Georgetown is without doubt impressive and distinctive. Of particular note is the use of timber, the most abundant and easily available building material. The physical aspects of the region and the social and historical context undoubtedly brought about the architecture that is seen in today's city. The influence of the European colonial powers, mainly the British, is immediately apparent in Guyanese architecture and town-planning, and features such as pitched roofs and porticoes with decorated pediments are clearly British colonial in nature. The layout of the city is a legacy of the Dutch engineers who designed it in such a way as to counteract its drainage problems. The decorative aspects of building and detailing evolved from southern European and Asian influences. These facets were brought together by the skilled local craftsmen of Guyana – all anonymous – to create graceful, elegant buildings.

It is clear that the houses expatriates were used to in their homelands, constructed in brick and stone, were radically different from those built by local Guyanese builders and craftsmen in Guyana. These men understood the country's climatic conditions and materials, although some colonial architects and builders who settled in Guyana, such as the Sharples family and H.O. Durham, developed an understanding of the local constraints just as well as the native builders. What they added was the decoration unique to Georgian and Victorian London, which was in turn derived from classical European architecture.

The architecture that developed in Georgetown would seem to be a natural adaptation of European culture to a different climate. We find elements of these buildings in plantation houses of the southern states of the USA, in the shingle style of New England, in the nineteenth-century buildings of the South African veld and in the houses of rural Australian towns. What they all have in common with those of Guyana is the source of their culture: British colonial presence.

As can be clearly seen in this book, in Georgetown this heritage is being swept away by the inevitable progress of modernization and the economics of conservation. Many of the

Redundant artisans' cottages huddle amid large-scale concrete developments in Kingston. The survival of the smaller cottages that make up the bulk of the old timber-built houses in Georgetown is now in question. The heritage tied up in these buildings is also being lost.

These buildings depict shelter at its most rudimentary in a tropical environment. The small cottage on the left is a miniature version of the great house with its pitched roof, sash window and window in the gable. The building below, although very basic, obeys the essential rule of building in Georgetown: it is elevated above the ground.

wooden buildings documented here are almost 150 years old. The most recent additions to the cityscape that correspond to the classic tradition of building are less than 100 years old. A combination of factors, among them the ravages of time, the shortage of appropriate materials and economic conditions, all play their part in the loss of these buildings.

There are encouraging signs, however. The government is now actively intervening by promoting grants and special status to encourage preservation in the private sector. The refurbishment and occupation of a number of wooden buildings in the city, undertaken by various government ministries and embassies, are stemming the tide of destruction. Indeed, the role of the Ministry of Culture has been instrumental in raising awareness of the case for conservation.

This cottage on Church Street appears to stretch along the street, but it is deceptive, since it is on a wide but shallow plot. The kitchen extension is on the far left, and there is a lean-to on the extreme right. The glazed sash windows on the main body of the house are fitted with side screens to protect the interior from the morning sun, which is strong even at 6 am, as the shadows in this photograph show.

The town houses on these pages have all survived, despite being adapted for various uses. The ground floor of the dwelling to the left has been filled in and is being put to commercial use. The building below retains its residential status, and is set in a landscaped garden.

This corner shop was obviously once a very elegant and well-proportioned house on stilts, and all its Demerara and sash windows are intact, despite the dilapidated appearance of the ground floor.

This building was the grandest of the set. Its front veranda, gable-end roof window and rear kitchen extension are all evident. Unfortunately, however, it is showing its age. The side panels and shade of the Demerara windows on the second floor have been removed, as have those on the first floor, facing the morning sun. They have been replaced by glass-panelled sash windows, so the house must become very hot inside. It now appears to be a multi-occupancy dwelling.

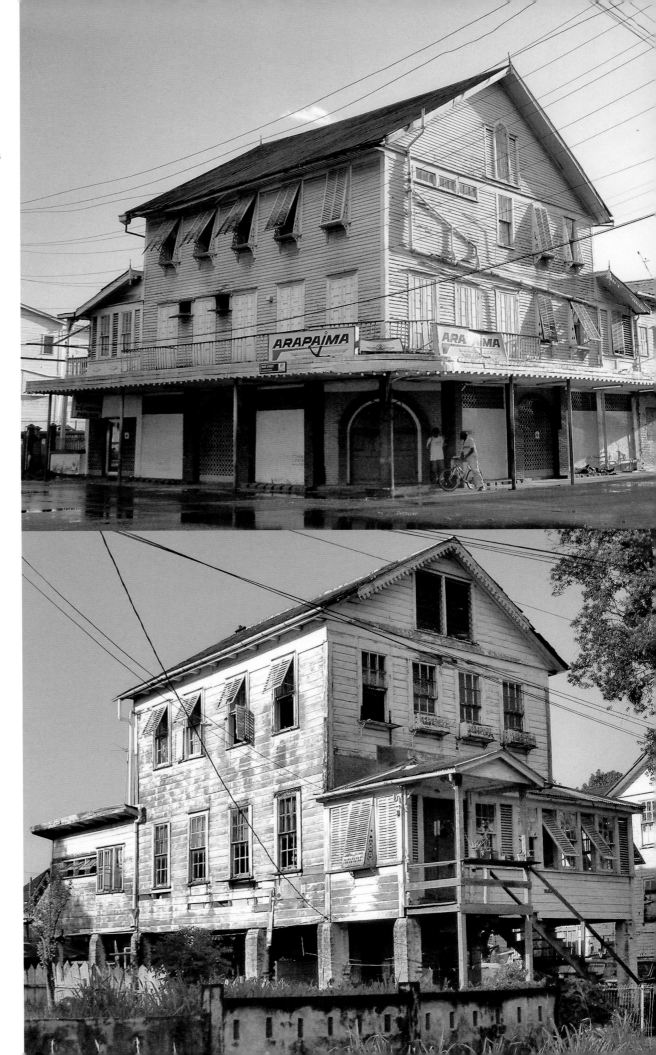

BIBLIOGRAPHY

A.W. Acworth, *Treasure in the Caribbean: A First Study of Georgian Buildings in the British West Indies*, London (Pleiades Books) 1949

G.W. Bennett, *An Illustrated History of British Guiana*, Georgetown (Richardson and Co.) 1866

Walter Brown, *Building for the Temperate Environment*, n.d.

Compton Dick, 'Formal Sector Housing in Guyana', University of Guyana, n.d.

Robert Fermor-Hesketh, *Architecture of the British Empire*, New York (Vendome Press) 1986

Thomas Fisher, 'The Well-Tempered Tropics', *Progressive Architecture*, 4/84 (1 April 1984), pp. 98–103

Hamilton Green, *Georgetown: An Anthology of Georgetown, Guiana and a Piece of the World*, Georgetown 2006

'Growth of Georgetown', www.guyana.org/features/guyanastory/chapter76.html, accessed 9 January 2017

Desmond Guinness and Julius Trousdale Sadler, *The Palladian Style in England, Ireland and America*, London (Thames & Hudson) 1976

Nicholas Guppy, *A Young Man's Journey*, London (John Murray) 1973

Sheik M. Hassan Aniff et al., *Historical Georgetown*, Georgetown (Sheik Hassan Productions) 2004

Henry Kirke, *25 Years in British Guiana* [1898], Boston, MA (Adamant Media Corporation) 2001

Latin America Bureau, *Guyana: Fraudulent Revolution*, London (Latin American Bureau) 1984

National Trust of Guyana, *Georgetown's Heritage Trail*, Georgetown (National Trust of Guyana) n.d.

Bonnie Ramsey, *Old Houses of the American South*, London (Thames & Hudson) 2000

Walter Rodney, *A History of the Guyanese Working People, 1881–1905*, Baltimore, MD (Johns Hopkins University Press) 1981

James Rodway, *History of British Guiana, from the Year 1668 to the Present Time*, Georgetown (J. Thomson) 1891

——, *The Story of Georgetown*, Georgetown (Argosy Co.) 1920

Vincent Roth, *A Life in Guyana, Volume 2: Later Years, 1923–1935*, Leeds (Peepal Tree Press) 2002

Barbara Savory, *A Guide to Georgetown City, Guyana*, Georgetown (Prime Time Advertising) 1996

Suzanne Slesin et al., *Caribbean Style*, New York (Clarkson Potter) 1985

Raymond T. Smith, *British Guiana*, London and New York (Oxford University Press) 1962

Rory Westmaas, 'Building Under Our Sun', in *Co-Operative Republic, Guyana 1970: A Study of Aspects of our Way of Life*, ed. Forbes Burnham and Lloyd Searwar, Georgetown (Guyana Lithographic) 1970

INDEX

ACKNOWLEDGEMENTS

This book has been many years in its gestation, from my early research as an architectural student at the then Polytechnic of Central London (PCL) in 1983, where tutors James Madge (head of department), Ed Winters and Eric Parry were instrumental in encouraging me with my thesis and started me on the road to producing this book. I would particularly like to thank my friends Helen Luck, Brian Smith, Jacqueline Clarke, Helen Cooper and Serena Thirkel for their encouragement and their invaluable support; Elizabeth Alderson for research and support; and John Agard and Grace Nichols for their help and encouragement. I greatly appreciated the encouragement of Frank Bowling, Rachel Scott and Spencer Richards to pursue this project. I am also very grateful to Wayne McWatt for his support and his extensive knowledge of Georgetown's houses, for assisting me to complete my research.

I would also like to acknowledge Sally Coffey, Stephen Bennett and particularly Kenny Laurenson, whose brilliance as an art director was much appreciated. They provided invaluable technical input as I developed my first ideas for this book.

In Georgetown the project met with great enthusiasm, and a great deal of assistance was given by Nirvana Persaud and Dr James Rose of the National Trust, who kindly lent me their map. The input of Lennox Hernandez of the Department of Architecture at the University of Guyana and the assistance of Syndrene Harris and Gwyneth George of the University Library service were also invaluable to my research.

This book could not have been completed without the immense feat of editing undertaken by Vicky Craver in compiling my first drafts. She encouraged my research to become meaningful and my text to come alive.

Frontispiece: This storm-damaged house in Queenstown stands in a once elegant but now unkempt garden. The front porch and steps have collapsed, but its original louvred and panelled gallery remains intact. The building fell further into dilapidation after this photograph was taken, and it was eventually demolished.

Page 4: A tower house in Main Street, Kingston.

Pages 6–7: A game of football is played with a backdrop of coconut trees and wooden colonial houses, looking from the eastern end of Croal Street across to Brickdam.

Page 8: House in Newmarket Street. The front gallery with its panelled windows is distinctive against the red of the main house.

Pages 10–11: Flamboyant trees in bloom on Thomas Street, looking towards Church Road. The outbuildings of Georgetown Hospital are on the left.

I would like to dedicate this book to my children,
Charlotte Phaure-Davis, Charles Davis and James Davis,
for their patience over the years in listening to my
stories about life in Guyana and viewing my
endless photographs of buildings.

Also to my grandson Elliot Ellmer-Phaure,
who is yet to have the pleasure of hearing these
stories and seeing these photographs.